Writing on the Walls at Night

Claudia Serea

CONTENTS

For Dana

*You should never hesitate to trade your cow
for a handful of magic beans.*

—*Tom Robbins*

I
THERE WERE NO MAGIC BEANS

PROLOGUE

The dark silhouette of a house pops up at the other end of the wheat field. The more I walk toward it, the more the field grows. Every blade has a hushed voice and a story to tell. They touch my legs as if begging me to listen. They offer me gold and poppies.

The sky is also a rippling wheat field with stories and voices. It's so much noise, how can I make them stop?

Everyone, hush! I tell them.

I sit criss-cross applesauce. Behind me, the house is lit and quiet in Grandma's kingdom.

Now I'm ready, I say. *Please speak one at a time.*

ALL WAS WELL IN HELL

Nothing to watch on TV but speeches. Large industrial
plants manufactured wooden clocks, tin birds, and bells with
no tongues. There was a 3-year waiting list for a car without gas.

We played outside all day with chalk and a ball. The key tied
around my neck jumped up and down and printed a dark bruise
on my chest. Lights off early in the entire cement city. Dear
comrades, we know you need your beauty sleep.

The Tooth Fairy was not allowed to fly behind the Iron Curtain.
Instead, my brother and I were visited by an old toothless fairy.
She limped into the room, stole the coins from the piggy bank,
and placed small potatoes under our pillows.

There was an endless invention fair, and we thought of the most
amazing things: the suitcase that would carry itself with a small
motor; the thermo-boots that would warm your soles in the deep
winter freeze; the toaster that would make sausage as well, and
eggs sunny-side-up, and arrange them into a smiley face on the
plate. *I love America*, you said. *When we go there, with all these
ideas, we'll be rich in no time.*

TONIGHT, THE RADIATORS SPEAK

Tonight, the radiators speak like birds. They chirp, sing, and trill. The pipes clang. Steam hisses and raps in slang. The house crackles and spits fire from its armpits. The birds inside the pipes take flight in my sleep.

This reminds me of a cold, cold, whitewashed room. So cold, I slept with gloves on. The ice on the window was thick, but I could still draw faces, a crooked garden, and a house with a roaring fire. I could hear the sleet slapping the cement. From my bed, I could smell the outside cold. All night, my breath wove a sheet of thin ice on the wall, on which women and men dressed in furs skated until morning.

The room of my childhood has a rug and a tall mirror. In the mirror, she's still there, curled on the red bed. She reads a book and blows into her hands to keep warm. Other times, she writes in her journal with frozen, calloused fingers.

She never laughs. I open the door, and she tells me: *Go away. I don't love you anymore. Why didn't you take me with you when you grew up?*

EVERYONE WAS STEALING EVERYONE ELSE'S HAT

Everyone was stealing everyone else's hat, and everything else we could: a bag of meat, a can of gas, a truckload of bricks. *Just redistributing*, we laughed. What's mine is mine. What's yours is still mine. Besides, who'd count the beans, the small potatoes, or the pig legs?

But we knew we'd be shot in the stadium if caught red-handed. What about magenta-handed, or maroon-handed? We passed by the guards, told them *Good evening*—we were so polite. We shook hands with them. Mine were pink; yours were orange; theirs were purple.

Mulberries and salt

I remember her mud and straw house with its open door through which old neighbor women who knew everything came unannounced. And its two mulberry trees, laden with dark fruit and caterpillars. We sat on the porch on kiddie chairs, watching the grapevine-covered yard and the road below.

The dusk kept falling for a long time. The chickens were pecking the pieces of history strewn everywhere, fallen mulberries and caterpillars mixed with dust and blood. Only we didn't know it was blood. Little bits of our previous lives gleamed in the dust.

In the kitchen, Grandma resembled a seventy-year-old Virgin Mary. Her back was hunched as if she carried the world bundled up under her dress. Her name was Maria, and she kept stirring something on the stove. She called me over to taste the stew. I gave her my necklace of salt tears to sprinkle in.

She prayed to God with fear and talked to Virgin Mary woman to woman, mother to mother. One old Virgin Mary to the other, younger one, perched over the bed, in an icon with large cloth wings. Maria asked for Mary's help. The icon was mute. A salt tear sparkled and fell into my hand like a pearl. Soon, I had enough for a new necklace.

A DONKEY, A CAMEL, A MARE:

Grandma carried me everywhere in the house on her back.
Giddy-up, Grandma! I sipped milk through a curly straw made
from her hair. In the dark, she carried me upstairs, my small
hands clasped around her neck. I couldn't see her face anymore,
but I knew I would never let go.

The cockroach looked at me. It moved its gigantic antennae and
wiggled its belly. I didn't dare cry, for my tears would have
brought it even closer. He could eat me, but not my little
brother. He was so small, a doll, sleeping. I could hear the
cockroach paws scratching the floor. *Hang on, little brother*, I
said. *I'll climb over you and protect you. When mother will unlock
the door, she'll find us embraced, smothered.*

My nose was a small bird that slept in a nest in Mother's hair.
I loved her scent of lilac and warm skin. So many years later,
summer rain falls like locks of hair over my face. There it is, the
faint lilac perfume. I sink into it, and inhale.

DEATH WEARS A CHEF HAT

The explosions are green and they happen in spring. First, the trees shoot up bullet-shaped buds, tight and glistening. The magnolia amasses fat grenades. The forsythia arms flame-throwers. At 5 a.m., when the robin gives the signal, they all detonate at once in tender green, white, pink, and blue: *Pow-pow, bang, ka-boom, ka-boom.*

Death wears a chef hat and prepares spring meals underground. On the menu, *foie gras* made from your liver and aspic from your knees. Your bones become soup that seeps through the stones. The grass drinks your voice through thousands of thin straws. I breathe the steam that vanishes in light, under a robin's wing: Grandma, are you making the robin sing?

In the kitchen, Mom listens to the radio and fills the jars with preserves. Preserve summer, when the little one was here. How she plucked the raspberries and plums from branches. How she opened her small mouth like a bird. Preserve that moment in a jar and place it on the pantry shelf next to the sealed bottles of oblivion.

The sea laughs at us and mixes our names with the names of the drowned. Her laugh sets wrinkles in sand and bores holes in rocks. She hides her mumbles in crevices and shells.

I smell danger in the salty wind. The poppies on the hill hide daggers in silk ruffles. Kiss me, but keep your hands away. I strapped a small knife to my thigh and I'm not afraid to use it.

Sweetheart, the tide is high; desire even higher.

THE TALL GLASS OF MILK ON THE TABLE

had white teeth ready to bite, a fully equipped maxilla under that inoffensive surface. I was afraid to swallow it, afraid those teeth would grow into my mouth.

Drink it! Mom commanded. Milk is hard to find. If it bites you, bite it right back.

Naked young women brush their hair glazed by the moon, and their hair becomes manes, and their hands become hooves. This is how summer arrives, my dear, in the gallop of white mares that trample the meadows and drink the dew.

History is written with gold letters, claimed the newspapers and the officials with cardboard mouths.

History is written with shit, Grandma said. She ripped the newspapers in thin long strips to hang on a rusty nail at the outhouse.

AT ATTENTION, EVERYONE WAS HOLDING THEIR BREATH

The generals were inspecting the troops again, and they could send you to jail for a missing button. The Great Powers were picking their great long noses. We lived like this a few decades. The only stir was that of the ants carrying home whatever they could steal from the fields.

The bells had wooden tongues, and so did the people. For the officials' visit, they replaced the live ducks on the pond with decoys. The air was full of sawdust pigeons, and the rivers, of driftwood fish. Everyone spoke a wooden language. We wore the words on a string around our necks. *Love* was a small carved cross. *Sadness*, a wooden spoon.

Love every day, said the fruit fly. The butterflies don't know what's written on their wings:
the *Life-is-surprisingly-short* ideogram.

I can tell you all about the revolution of the flies. They stained the photo of the beloved leader in the newspaper that lined the table. Oh, the crowds, the spattering of sauce! The grease running across the printed page! In the kitchen, history was made. You can read it all in the stains on the wall.

Only the mess survives.

The Caterpillars

The caterpillars kept me company. They lived in the two mulberry trees and munched on the leaves. At night, I heard their crunch and rustle until they crawled into my dreams.

In the collective, Grandma fed the mulberry leaves to the silkworms. Time was fuzzy and spun days of raw silk. Nights were cocoons.

A furry flood, they climbed the walls. They covered the table and chairs with moving lace. The little girl crouched in a corner. She wanted to be a caterpillar, too. Her only chance was to weave a cocoon and hang under the bed.

The silkworms got sick and died in the summer. The caterpillars invaded the porch. The mulberry trees' purple blood stained the dirt beneath them.

My brother and I picked the silken mulberries from the ground and ate them, then spoke with black tongues. Once, instead of a mulberry, he swallowed a piece of black and glistening chicken shit. To this day, he feels very lucky.

Luck is something you ingest or step into. Sometimes, it's a beautiful woman wearing a flame dress and turning the corner. But most of the time, it's just the byproduct of pigeons. *Make me lucky, Mother, then throw me into the fire.* And she did.

SOMETIMES I CAN'T FALL ASLEEP
BECAUSE OF THE NOISES

Once, I swallowed my tooth, and the Tooth Fairy reached inside me to grab it.

I had a huge collection of shoes, all kinds, multicolored and flickering, like butterflies. It was worth millions. The queen stole it from me and inspected each shoe for specks of dust.

Just then, Prince Charles burst in, dragging behind a grandfather clock. He gave it to me and I ran into it, tickety-tock. My name was Glamourdiva, and I was a mouse on top of Big Ben. The huge arms moved over the world until they struck twelve and the cuckoo came out.

The bus pulls in. Inside it, small children hang from the straps like piglets in the smoker. Each time a child boards the bus, comrade teacher snatches them and hangs them up. We're next in line. I'm trying to get Mom's attention, but she's busy talking on the phone.

 Hanging room only, the bus driver says, and we step back. The bus closes the doors and drives away.

A shiny orange caterpillar crawls across the ceiling. Someone is creeping up the stairs. I can hear his breath and the creaks in the wood floor.

I can't fall asleep even after three bedtime stories. Next to me, Mom snores softly. The wind and rain outside cover up the noise of the footsteps.

The evening report

What did you do today? Did the butcher sell you a pig's ear wrapped in bloody newspaper? Did you tell him how you're going to cook it? Was it the news about our town? Have you read the dissident writing in the clouds? With whom did you discuss it? Beware, the walls are perked-up ears. The spider in the corner watches and listens when you talk to yourself.

At sundown, the field mice, the moles, and prairie dogs abandon the earth. Armies of rodents invade the sky. They chew and dig and grind. They multiply and squeak. Look up, dear: the maze of burrows and tunnels spreads overhead. The ground is hollow under our feet. The sky is hollow, too, dotted with mounds of luminous dirt: road maps traced by rodents.

We laughed like in the old times. You leaned against a pine tree I never saw before in my yard. When I looked closer, you *were* the pine tree. Scraggly, half-dry, and dirty, your body was devastated by chemicals and drought. You bent and dipped your branches into the clear pool. The water filled with pine needles and mud.

What will I do now with all this dirty water?
I'm sorry, you said. *I just had to clean up a bit.*

Your branches now looked greener, dripping. You smiled, and small pink blooms opened on the climbing rose behind you.

The damned are restless again, but they've been labeled a terrorist group. The bus drivers from River Styx Transit are still on strike. There are new tax hikes, and the crime rate is on the rise. The small dog of the earth bites off the noses and ears of corrupt politicians, but it could only do so much. Thank you for watching the underworld news. Good night.

No one notices

1.

Evening is an old woman who has Mom's sunburned face. She wears a dress of chamomile and smoke. She sows stars in the plum trees and lights plums in the sky.

She turns on the crickets and the news. Night after night, we listen to the same words. No one notices when vines and leaves cover the TV screen. The anchors' heads grow into melons.

Old-woman evening passes by the windows and lights up talking melon heads in every home.

2.

In her dress of fog and coffee, the dawn steps barefooted into the world. She, too, has my mother's face, but no one notices.

She harvests stars from the plum trees and turns off plums in the sky. She switches on the traffic and the morning news. She picks up talking melon heads from the garden and serves them for breakfast.

History is what we take in, Mom says, the small bites of the present. *Eat up, dear. It's all on the table in front of you.*

SHITVILLE

In the woods, crows peck the daylight until it's gone, gone, gone. Only a few nickels of sun remain scattered under the trees, for the Gypsy girls to find and string into necklaces.

The Gypsy quarters are called Shitville because of the houses of mud and dung. Here, the fires burn day and night, with little kids roasting on pits. The bears are bony and the horses have eyes full of flies. Everyone seems to be asleep, so I run, jumping over large burr leaves and the green hair of the ferns.

I catch my breath next to a house with a patch of corn.
A woman voice calls my name from inside: *Come to baba,*
little bird, so I can read your future in the corn seeds.
But I don't want to know my future, and I run, run, run.

THERE WERE NO MAGIC BEANS

There were no magic beans, but everyone had a magic beanstalk
made of copper wire. It grew from the radio, curled around the
radiator, across the room, up to the ceiling, and through the
roof. Each day, I climbed it all the way to
      Munich and West Berlin.

Ich bin ein Berliner, said the handsome president.
Yeah, we all were, behind the tall walls where his speech never
      made it.

It's easy to talk now, but what did you do then?

I climbed the beanstalk and listened to rock music. Illegal stuff,
you know, like hot sticky sweet rationed sugar. I envied the polka
dot crocodile who somehow managed to smuggle a request to
the radio station and dedicated the song to his high school
sweetheart, the princess with the heart of broken glass.

At night, I used a dream sharpener. With the dream's pointed
tip, I drew a window in the wall and escaped.

SÂNZIENE

This is the night when the girls wash their faces with dew, and watch how the gates of the world open, and the spirits let them see their future. This is the night when all the animals, insects, and birds can talk, and you can hear them. It's the night when the sky grove changes, and the sun starts getting smaller. At midnight, summer and winter hang in balance on a knife blade, with all the weather, winds, and stars before summer recedes. In the midnight stalls, winter breeds its stallions.

This is the night to pick miraculous herbs: chicory gives strength; white fern flower makes you lucky all year; maple leaves heal wounds and headaches; *măselarita* cures toothaches and makes you light, so you can fly on a broom; snakeweed blooms at midnight and disappears the next day, so catch it before it's gone and use it for a love spell. If you're brave enough to swallow it, you can touch anyone and read their fate like an open book. And don't forget verbena and *zarna*, the love weeds.

At midnight, naked in the moonlight, pick the *sânziene* flowers and hang them in the window to chase away the ghosts and the undead. Wear them around your waist to make your womb as fertile as summer. Burn them to burn the devil. Braid wreaths and throw them on the roof. This is the night to peer into your future. If the wreaths cling to a tile, you'll get married this year.

V FROM VICTORY

In your presence, my thoughts draw a V shape, a flock of storks in the sky. *V from victory*, you say. I try calling them back, telling them they got it all wrong. They should draw an S from *surrender*, but they don't listen. My thoughts are gone south for the winter, and you smile. Your mouth draws a V from victory on your face, or a U from *I can't believe u fell for it*.

You shouldn't have your head in the clouds all the time, Mom said. But what if I were a really tall giraffe, or a weather balloon? What if I were the Pink Panther followed everywhere by a raincloud? I'd rather carry a cloud in my head than all these thoughts about what I should or shouldn't do.

Night and day, the crow and the seagull fly over the sea. The crow brings warships to my door. With a swish, the seagull turns them into fishing boats. Armies of fish move swords in the transparent water. I open the door to steps in sand. Tell me: are you gone fishing or off to war?

The woman in the moon sings and combs swallows from her hair. The swallows bring little bits of spring on Earth in their beaks. They stick it with mud and saliva in a corner of Mom's porch. They land on the clothesline and brag about their mansions on the moon. *The nests are too narrow here,* they say. *The moon is much larger.*

Mom hears them, looks up and waves at the other woman in the sky, then keeps on singing and combing her hair.

Yes, my body shifts shape when emotions change. When you kiss me, my fingers catch fire like matches. I turn my face into black squid ink when I want to hide. I flip the switch again and it's morning, sunny and bright. I'm in your arms. My hair fills the room with a lilac grove in bloom.

THE LONGEST TRIP

I stopped trying to understand why it snowed every time I
thought of you. Dressed in our best clothes, we were stuck for
hours on a train in the middle of the snowed-in field. We played
charades with the shapes of the wind.

At noon, we caught a bus that only got us as far as the road was
plowed. We walked in our long coats and fur hats, a snowman
and a snowwoman. When we got tired, we sat on the side of the
road and ate frozen sandwiches. Your hand was hot in mine.

Later, we were picked up and traveled on top of a horse-drawn
wagon full of corn stalks, then in the back of a car that delivered
fresh bread. I had a long blizzard veil; you had a white carnation
boutonnière. The weatherman said, *You may kiss the bride.*

EVERYONE WANTS TO RUN AWAY

Let's run away, love. Let's fly faster than the incoming storm.
My back burns. The eyes of our chasers pierce holes in my side.
Throw the hairbrush, love. Where it touches the ground, the
woods will grow behind us, and we'll hide.

Let's run, love. Let's fly like demons set loose by a curse. My
body hurts from the dog bites. Love, throw the knife behind us.
Where it falls, a mountain will rise, and we'll escape.

Let's run love. Let's fall into the deep together. My hair is on fire,
and I hear our hunters' boots. We're close to the border, dear,
and the patrol has orders to shoot. Throw my scarf behind, love.
The Danube will stretch as far as we can see. The soldiers will
sink into its hungry mouth, and we'll be free.

WHEN I PRESSED ENTER

A tiny trap door opened in the keyboard. The stairs were going down into the endless cellar. It was full of roots and spiders. I grabbed the flashlight and a pocketful of pebbles so I could find the way back to my room. On the other side of the trap door it said RETURN, but I knew I wouldn't be back soon.

Everyone's name was written in the *Book of Rain*. When we read it, the Nor'easter blew harder, blurring our silhouettes. We were walking home from the edge of the world in the thick crosshatch of the rain. Covered by lines, your face dissolved, and I could barely hear your voice: Hurry up, the book is closing! And we ran as fast as we could and jumped into the book before it closed with a thunder. We were the last two names
on the wet dustcover.

II

THE KEEPERS OF MOON KEYS

DEAR READER,

I'm one of them. I was born at 8 p.m., a night creature.
I hang out with the weird ones, the poets, the lunatics,
the ones who babble, who talk to themselves like the wind, or
the rain. Before turning the page, stock up on salt, garlic, and
wooden stakes. I'm from Romania—can you see my fangs?

LONG AGO, THE BREAD LADY, THE MILK LORD, AND THE PRINCE OF PICKED BONES

ruled the kingdom. There was no bread, no milk, and no bone to be picked, but, for a while, the people kept dreaming about them. One night, the Bread Lady, the Milk Lord, and the Prince of Picked Bones stepped into our dreams and took everything they could. Since then, the shelves have been empty. There was no bread, no milk, and no bone to pick. Not even in a dream.

THE HEDGEHOG TALKS TO THE BEE ABOUT GOD

What do you mean, he has a little bit of dirt left? And he doesn't know what to do with it? What kind of God is he if he doesn't know?

And why did he send you to me? He wants *me* to tell *you* what to do with the dirt? How much dirt are we talking about? A few crumbs? No? A lot??

And why is he asking *me*? He made me so ugly and full of spikes, and now he wants my advice? And I can't even charge by the hour?

Let me get this straight: he made the whole entire world, and now he can't think by himself to make some hills and mountains out of the leftover dirt? He can't think to make the man just like him? He never heard of a self-portrait?

So what if he gets it wrong? What happens when God gets the man wrong? Well, how would I know, bee? How would I know?

THE KEEPERS OF MOON KEYS

Gigi was a tall pale man who drove an invisible truck through
my hometown. He revved, blasted the horn, and switched gears,
running down the street at maximum speed. His brakes squealed
when he pulled into the bus stop and offered free rides to
everyone. *Come with me, I know the way,* he said, and
I believed him.

Maria had a ravaged nest for hair. One day, she came to school
and offered all the teachers sour cherry preserves from a jar. The
cherries were bright red and glistened like her lipstick. *Eat up!* she
yelled, cramming full teaspoons into the teachers' mouths.
*Today is my son's birthday, the one I lost ten years ago. Here's a
spoonful of cherries to sweeten his soul.*

There is a man who runs naked down the street, even in
wintertime. Sometimes he rides a bike, carrying bags stuffed with
newspapers. He collects yesterday's news. No one talks to him or
stops him. Undisturbed, he rides and babbles, ringing the bell. I
heard his name is Mr. Truth.

Every town has a keeper of moon keys. They remember what didn't happen and mumble the names of the dead. At night, they stroll into dreams. I hear the brakes of the invisible truck down the street, the bike's bell and newspapers rustle, and the ping of the teaspoon in the jar with preserves—and I know the moon keys are safe.

Baba Marina

Baba Marina lived in our attic. When our family moved, she moved in with us. She'd throw a fit otherwise. When the old village moved in the new location, Baba Marina moved, too. She didn't like to be by herself in the attic. One night, when Mother couldn't sleep, she got up and went to the kitchen. And there was Baba Marina peeling potatoes and the eyes of the dead, throwing them into the boiling pot. In the morning, Mother's hair was white as if she had walked through falling snow.

ZARAZA

I want you to tell me, beautiful Zaraza, who are the ones who
loved you? How many have cried for you
and how many have died?

—Cristian Vasile, Zaraza

You set my heart on fire, Zaraza, princess of slums! You set my
heart on fire—this old house burns to the ground when you
dance on its roof. And everyone can see your thighs, your
billowing black pantyhose.

You set my heart on fire, Zaraza, this house of cinder and debris
where no one lives. I can't bear to see you dance flamenco with
the flames, pirouette through sparks and leap into the green
devil's arms.

How many houses have you burned? How many men have you
gorged? How many lives have you wilted with your smile?

Gypsy woman, my heart has turned to ashes, and I just want
to taste your lips—do they taste of lilies or lies? I just want to
touch your skin—does it smell of night or sin?

And, when you'll die, I'll drink your ashes, Zaraza, brown sugar in my coffee, one teaspoon at a time.

THE COLLECTOR OF CLOUDS

The collector of clouds sips tea in his blue penthouse and watches the gathering storms. He's always on the lookout for funnels. He uses cloud computing to keep track of the shapes. He keeps his treasures in transparent boxes labeled with beautiful Latin names. He sends his emissaries all over the world to get the latest Nimbus creations. Come, take a look, he gestures. My mirrors are full of angels, and rain clouds are cheap. And here are my rarest pieces: the antique Cumulus with its silver lining and the elusive Cloud 9.

Aunt Suzie and the village

In the dead of winter, there wasn't much to do and no TV to watch, so I took up crocheting. I crocheted replicas of all the people in the village: of Aunt Suzie, Old Man Gheorghe, my neighbor Lulu, my cousin Elena reading a crocheted book, the priest, the policeman, Baba Marina, the ghost from the cemetery, everyone. I crocheted their eyeglasses, headscarves, clothes, their cheeks and lips, their hair.

I crocheted Aunt Suzie's dog from brown, fuzzy yarn and her flock of geese from feathery white and gray threads. And, when Aunt Suzie died, I crocheted her organs from bright red and brown silk, and her skeleton, complete with ivory teeth, floppy ribs, and soft phalanges. I crocheted her brain, ruffled and creased with all her cloudy yarn thoughts and convoluted synapses.

I assembled her body on the dining room table, each organ nestled in a crinkly silk sack. The heart was the last to go in, knotted and intricate, with all the blood threads laced through the body. People said I had too much time on my hands, but what do they know?

51

I told them, Fate crochets us all the time with colorful threads. She links the day with the night, mother with child, spring with summer with fall with winter, and life with death: one loop, slip stitch, chain, turn, join two stitches, repeat. She drives her hook through my brother and me, and we both hang by a thread. Then by another. Loop, stitch, chain. Repeat. Fate has too much time on her hands.

THE GRAVEDIGGER'S DAUGHTER

On the clothesline in the clouds, the gravedigger's daughter
hangs kilims, bed sheets, blouses, and flowered tablecloths out to
dry. No reason to cry at the graves. The souls have all gone up
already. They flap overhead in the wind, in the empty
shirtsleeves.

She comes to my window without a sound. Her face is white
with petroleum eyes. Her cold hands reach into my lover's body
and grab the heart. It's red and shiny and it shivers. She gives it to
me, so now I carry two hearts: my own, and another one, the
smallest, most radiant heart, glowing all night.

THE WOMAN WITH WHITE CLOUD HAIR

In the house of lace and sepia photos lives a woman with white cloud hair. She wears a bomber high up in her hair cloud. The pilot is her lover, always on her mind. On the papered wall, a clock in a cloud among clocks and clouds ticks his time away from her.

All night, I tried on huge Russian hats. So tiring. I tried long fur coats, large animal skins, and towering hats so heavy I couldn't move. I went for a walk, but there was no path, just freshly-dug dirt clinging to my boots, making them even heavier. Then the earth parted, and I almost fell in murky waters. I grabbed a tree limb and pulled myself out, soaking wet from the cold river. My long, wet fur coat was so heavy I couldn't carry it, so I let it go. My Russian hat had fallen. Good riddance, I said, and headed out of there.

The end of the world dragged on. All night, she smoked with the door open. In the yard, spring was limping, a man walking back home after the war.

TANTI MARIANA

She was born old and waiting. In summer, the tears not yet spilled pool inside her chest. In fall, she fingers a rosary of rain.

Tonight, I'm sending you the sand between my breasts, the rain from my pillow, and the darkness between my thighs in a perfumed envelope that will tremble in the mailman's hand. I'm stuffing it with thousands of verses written by entwined dragonflies, and the romance novel of the clouds kissing shamelessly. When you'll receive it, you'll know what to do: hop on the next plane, wild goose, or thunderbolt, love, 'cause I'm wilting here waiting for you.

But he never came back. In winter, all her tears dried and the empty riverbeds froze. Her soul was a cave with a stalagmite at its center. One drop kept falling, and her sadness built up but never reached the surface.

The surface broke in spring when the river burst free. As waters carried her tears into the sea, her body became smaller and smaller.

The bone music maker

The bone music maker is a bootlegger of jazz and rock and roll. His name is Sasha and he lives on Resurrection Street. Each week, he looks for X-rays in the hospital dumpsters and takes them home to turn them into records. The hospitals are full of sick people. The dumpsters overflow with X-rays. And banned music is nowhere to be found.

Sasha presses the music into the X-rays with a machine and cuts the disks with scissors. He burns a hole in the center with his cigarette and holds up the result to light: Elvis's *Heartbreak Hotel* on the ribs. Johnny Cash's *I Walk the Line* on metatarsals and phalanges. Miles Davis on pneumonia. Chuck Berry on the broken hip. Dizzy Gillespie on Uncle Misha's brain tumor. Ready for the turntable for just 1 ruble.

They sound like voices through torrential rain, ghosts singing through static. Like music in fog, light years away. Piano and trumpets played by the bees. *Rontgenizdat* is criminal and everyone knows it. But students donate blood to get the money to buy bone music.

Someone must have ratted on Sasha. One day, the Komsomol Music Patrol raided the apartment and confiscated everything: the piles of X-rays, the records still unsold, even the manicure scissors and the cigarettes he smoked and used to burn the record holes. Some say Sasha hid in the empty coffin waiting for Uncle Misha in the dining room. Others say he went to prison and another bone music maker took his place.

In any case, on Resurrection Street, on skulls, vertebrae, and femurs, the banned bone music lives on. And the bones shake, rattle, and roll.

THE MAN WHO PAINTS THE TIME

He's inside the clock in the airport. Only the hour hand is painted in. The man dips his brush in the paint can and traces a long black line, uniting the center of the clock with the figure 12. Now the clock has a minute hand.

He's tall and handsome, although I can't see his face. He cleans the glass surface with a squeegee. Oblivious to all the passengers, he bends and washes a rag in the bucket. Up again, he wipes off the black minute hand he just painted. The passengers look at each other: what is this guy doing inside the clock? And why did he wipe off the minute hand?

The man washes the rag in the bucket. If you ever wonder where does the time go, well, let me tell you: it's in the white bucket. He notices a speck left on the clock's surface and cleans it up with his sleeve. Unhurried, he loads his brush with black paint and slowly paints a new long line from the center to the right of the figure 12. It's one minute after 12.

The passengers are captivated. He ignores everyone and makes sure the black minute hand is perfect, with no wavy edges. He's taking his time—he's a perfectionist, that's why. Then, with quick moves, he wipes the line with the squeegee. What happened? It wasn't straight enough? What a waste of time. The man next to me returns to his paper, mumbling.

I get up and circle behind the huge clock. No one is there. There is no stair, no door. The clock is so thin no one could fit inside. Back in the waiting room, I take my seat and look up: there he is, absorbed in his task, painting another minute.

THE WOODS' OLD HAG AND OTHER WINGED CREATURES

The earth parches under her steps. Villages burn. Cities crumble. She rides the midnight wind, her face a rotten hollow rock. She has a forest for hair and howls like the storm. She eats the children who don't listen to their parents. She wanted to eat me too, but I escaped riding a fly.

She sits by the fire roasting a small animal skewered on a stick. They say she eats children, but it can't be true. *Eat*, she says, and hands me a piece of meat with tiny bones. It could be a frog's leg, or a young chicken's.

 It's the peace dove, she explains when I hesitate.

 Don't worry, no one will miss it. It tastes delicious.

The mother eagle carried me on its back away from the dark valley. The gnarled river below was chewing rocks and lives. Every time the eagle turned its head, I fed it a hunk of beef and a loaf of bread. I finished the 40 pieces of meat and 40 breads right at the mouth of the precipice.

The eagle turned its hungry beak again. I sliced my buttock and pushed it into its beak.

Ooooh, dear, the mother eagle said. *Your flesh is so sweet, I almost wanna gulp you and forget you saved my life.*

How do you get a horse with seven hearts, quick as the wind? You have to guard seven wild mares for seven nights. Don't lose them, or your neck will meet the wooden stake that's singing for a head. If you succeed, the old witch will let you choose a mare. She'll hide the hearts of the six others into the skinniest wobbly horse. Choose wisely, that's all I'm saying.

JUANITA, THE TEJU LIZARD

My name is Juanita, and this is my second life, reincarnated as John Barrale's cowboy boots. The boots are beautiful as I was once: soft skin, delicate pattern, and an irreverent heel that kicks ass.

Oh, but these are not just any beautiful boots. They're blessed with the magic of poetry. I, Juanita, the Teju lizard, was once the poetess and priestess of the desert. Now, I'm John's muse. Who knows where poetry comes from? In the wild, it comes from the movement of the stars, or from the immobility of the rocks. If you're a poet, like John, poetry might flow from your boots.

Tonight, John picks up the pair, and I know it's a special occasion. He shines them, and I feel the love of his hands. He puts them on and walks with a spring in his step. Here are the poems, John, oozing from the lizard boots, sent by me, Juanita. Go on, John. Dazzle everyone at your poetry reading, and ride off into the sunset. And, as they say, *¡Mucha mierda!*

THE LARGE MOTH THAT FLEW IN

It poked me in the cheek, trying to fly into my mouth, seeking
refuge as if it were a word I uttered a long time ago and now
awakened from the dead.

Moth, from Old English *moththe*, Middle Dutch *motte*, Old
Norse *motti*—were you a sound from sleep, a muffled cry? Were
you spoken in error in the wrong ear, unintelligible, soft? Were
you lost, looking for meaning down my throat?

Were you the comet moth, the black witch, the luna or the
Gypsy, the emperor's gum, good god, the dark dagger, dusky
brocade, the death's hand, the flame, the ghost, the shark, the
snout, or the true lover's knot? Were you November, or winter?
Were you a message from the dead?

I'll never know. I picked you up and threw you out
into the night.

Amy Eats Men for a Snack

Amy eats men for a snack. She carries them in a Ziploc bag, dips them in ranch dressing, and munches on them like carrots. Mmmm, tasty. I can hear the crunch from across the room. It makes me want to eat some, too.

On Pont des Arts, they locked their love forever and threw the key in the river. *We'll never part*, they swore. *Eternity will find us embraced like the padlock that hugs the bridge railing with metal strength.* Unless, of course, the bridge collapses under the weight of the locks. The maintenance crew rushes to clean up the mess *vite, vite*. Someone named Jean-Paul carries their love away in a wheelbarrow full of rusty padlocks and throws it in the city's metal recycle bin.

Amy paints her lips a glistening red. She smiles all the time. By smiling, she disguises her feelings. She could work in customer service. She could answer the phone in a smiling voice or greet the guests at the door:

Hi, my name is _____. How may I help you today?

Even at night, Amy smiles, a disguise for her dreams. She doesn't give anything away. Her lips keep mum. She smiles at the world, and no one knows what she hides.

Sometimes she doesn't feel like talking. She goes an entire day without saying a word. Like a lizard in the desert, her skin turns the color of sand, and she becomes a chameleon perfectly camouflaged in the color of silence. She listens to the sound of her own thoughts, the way the lizard listens to the sound of sand grains rolled by wind. Millions and millions of sand grains on the move. If she keeps quiet long enough, she can hear the sand dunes shifting shape. By the next day, the landscape has changed, and she starts speaking again.

October dips the maple trees in cold air and turns them into candied apples. Amy licks the brilliant red. Sunshine syrup glazes the street outside the deli where she buys a fruit salad. *I can't stand that much sweetness*, she tells the girl at the counter. The girl smiles at her with rotten teeth.

THE SPIDER STRINGS BEADS AND SEQUINS
ON SILK THREADS

She stitches the days with the nights into a dress. She spins, pulls, weaves; she knits long sleeves for winter nights; short pleats, winter sleet; long veils, summer haze; and small pearl buttons for her naps. When the life dress is done, she places it on a wire hanger and hangs it from the crescent moon.

The boy climbs the spiral staircase inside his mother's ear. The steps are made of cast iron, tight and intricate, and he can only go up, up to the white cloud. Far away, his mother's dreams fly above the field, a flock of cranes calling, searching, before heading to warmer climates.

MEANWHILE, IN ROMANIA

The Lord of Meanwhile meets me for dinner in a restaurant named The Snows of Yesteryear. An angel-robot bicycles by the door, lighting up the plasma lamp in her head. She wears a golden gas mask and murmurs: *Follow me, please.*

The bartender pours vanishing cocktails in our glasses. Waiters walk backwards, carrying trays they fill with food from the tables. Our server is named Snowden, and he recommends the fleeting duck confit and the fugitive caviar.

On the walls, cog insects open and close their stiff wings. Birds made of keys fly on the ceiling. Steel tulips bloom in corners, and the huge clock mechanism turns, turns, turns its hour and minute arms.

What kind of place is this? I ask. The Lord of Meanwhile smiles and doesn't say anything. We sip our vanishing year drinks. The robot angel returns and says: *Time is a machine like any other.*

Self-portrait

Claudia is
to a cloud

as chalk is
to chocolate.

III

DARK CALLIGRAPHY

THE MUSEUM IS CLOSING, THE CUSTODIAN SAID

A girl walks through the torn city saying her silent goodbyes. She touches the walls with her fingertips.

Farewell, fences. Goodbye, sweets shop selling cakes dripping with syrup and caramel squares hard as bricks. So long, schoolyard where she tore her knees roller skating. See you later, *Cornus* tree covered in golden flowers and bees.

*

Rooms filled with hanged people. Rooms filled with relics and bones. Rooms filled with old artifacts salvaged from fire and bombs. There is hardly a place to sit among the memories, so, please stand. Place your hand over your heart and face the past.

*

In the blown-up building at the corner, a chair leans against the void. Photos still cling to the walls, men and women with funny glasses and moustaches. Some have bonnets, others, top hats, and they all walk arm in arm to the edge of the frames.

*

Big red stars perched like predatory birds on the buildings and on the shoulders of men in uniforms. Big hammers hung on the streets, next to big bunches of wheat. The big drums started to beat when the men spoke.

*

On the cement wall,
light doesn't reveal a door,
but a wrought-iron shadow
of a gate.

Inside, an old woman makes the bed
as if waiting for a visitor.

*

Meanwhile, three geese ask the clouds for direction. How do they align so perfectly in formation? Who goes first at the arrowhead? Who gets to be last? How do they know which way to fly, and where is North? Do they look at us from above and marvel at the swarming? Do they show us a sign in the sky, how to find the road back home through the winter?

*

Let's dance!
The days are getting shorter
and children grow so quickly,
just with water.

One-two-three,
pirouette through the years,
small shoes next to large ones.

One-two-three,
little darling,
let's dance with the leaves

before the statues cry
and crumble,

before the lake shrugs
our memories away.

*

One day, a blue and green fly landed on her parents' photo, the one in which they tried kissing just after getting married, but they burst into laughter instead. The fly rubbed its tiny paws dipped in dust, writing something unintelligible onto the frame. A message?

*

Mayhem, the cat, knows the way:

tip-
toe on
the roof,

around the ledges,
close to
the pigeon coop.

*

Silence, heavy with secrets. The past is filled with silence and smoke, but the scent of the fire still talks. The custodian turns the key and walks home.

*

In the empty room,
the striped uniforms hang
from hooks in the ceiling.

Now they are filled only with air.
The breeze moves them,
turns them,

so we can see them better
in the naked light,

the hanging uniforms
of the dead.

DARK CALLIGRAPHY

On the blank sheet of paper,
the little girl writes
a row of letters *t*.

Her pen screeches,
barely audible,
against the white,

as she slowly fills
the vast field of the page.

*

Rooms filled with silence: a museum, a library, a classroom with
kids taking a test. We move from room to room, silence to
silence: from the empty church to the ICU, to the closed bar, to
the deserted hallway where a janitor mops the floor.

There is the silence of a still life, the silence of Monet's water
lilies, and, in my mother's house, the silence of the plastic flowers

in a vase. But my favorite silence is the one of the snow when the twigs draw their dark calligraphy.

*

Is it better to know,
or not know?

To remember,
or not?

To notice,
or glide by,

closing your eyes
at the ruins of the buildings
where we were supposed to line up
by the hundreds to receive
our daily soup?

*

Snow and silence, the enemies. Snow falls, covering everything, making it feel alright. No matter what it is, it will be covered by snow, including and accepting all in silence. Let's bury the past,

it says. Let's cover the mass graves with an immaculate silence, a
sheet pulled over the dead. Let's throw away the shovels.

*

Overnight, it snowed
and silence covered everything.

Even the crows were quiet.

Only the woodworms kept chewing
the furniture and walls.

Not everyone could hear them, though.

My grandfather and a few others could,
and they were driven mad
by the deafening chew.

Sooner or later,
everything will crumble, they said,
but no one believed them.

*

The little girl had finished her homework and left the paper on the table in the deserted kitchen. Row after row, the white field of her sheet was filled with slanted dark crosses. Outside, the wind was tracing its own calligraphy in the trees.

The Warhorses

I want to tell you about the horses, how they galloped, pulling
our wagon to the end of the world, from where we walked back.
And how the fog whispered to the young trees. *Don't worry.
You'll see much of the world go by and still get your rings if you
bend in the wind just a little.*

My grandfather liked horses and went to war with the logistics
unit, the lucky kitchen corporal. When the front fell at
Stalingrad, he ran out of the kitchen wearing only a shirt, but
they didn't have room for him in the truck. *You can ride on the
cannon*, they said. 2,000 miles, 2 weeks in February at minus 40
degrees, embracing the cannon lady for dear life. When they got
to Romania, they pried him away from the metal flesh: stiff,
teeth clenched, eyes swollen like beets. They sent him home
to die.

At home, grandmother Stefana bathed him in oats and wrapped
his head in hot barley bandages. She boiled the horse feed and
packaged him in grain, a mummy in the darkest room of the
house. She changed the gauze and fed him oatmeal with a
teaspoon. She hummed a little song and whispered a prayer:

Virgin Mary,/ Mother of God,/ bring back my man/ with a white horse heart. Two months later, in spring, he opened his eyes.

This is how we play this game: you tell me a story about a man and his horses. I tell you a story about another man and his horses. Through our veins, dark wine horses pull a wagon into the night.

My other grandfather went to war on the Eastern Front with his own horses. 158,000 Romanians died in the field where the river Don elbows its way into Stalingrad. My grandfather was taken prisoner and sent to Siberia where only blizzard horses graze. From there, he was sent to fight to the West in front of the Red Army, up to the Tatra Mountains in Central Europe. At the end of the war, he came home on foot. All the horses were dead when he got to his village, so he bought a bicycle.

A husband is like a horse, Grandmother said. Give him good food, fresh water, and a handful of hay, and he'll always come home.

On the battlefields of the world, the grass grows straight out of the bones beneath. The horses graze on the hair of the dead and look at me with thoughtful eyes. I hear their lips ripping the grass blades. The horses don't move; they only twitch their skin and swish their tails. After the armies leave, these are the sounds that history makes: the crunching, the chewing, the faint buzzing of the flies, and the tails swishing them away.

BLACK TIE AFFAIR

On the charred field, clouds of crows arrive looking for leftovers.
The field is littered with debris, a scorched battleground
scattered with bits of wood and bones, as after an explosion.
   What happened here? I ask. *Who died?*
   Was it my father before he was my father?
The crows don't answer. They stare at me, preening their suits
and silk black ties.

For years, I walked with my raven through the desert. He was
very quiet and soft. He listened to everything I said, looking at
me with black button eyes. I tied a string to him and walked with
him through endless mountains and valleys. We slept in caves
under the sky full of windblown bed sheets.

Give me water, says the black heart in the ground. Give me rain,
give me sun. Keep me moist and warm, deep in the earth. And
I'll grow for you sunflowers and milkweeds. I'll caress your soles
with grasses and your hands with leaves. I'll feed you berries and
grapes. If you'd only give me your water and sun, give me your
sweat, the skin that you shed, give me your dust, your hair,
your flesh, your bones, gimme—gimme—gimme!

THE NAMES

1.

Trains, trains, trains chew the night with steel teeth.
Cattle trains crowded with names:
Maria, Ioana, Stefana, Gheorghe, Ion, Constantin.
Trains loaded with souls, some moaning, some silent,
taking them to the end of the world.

What is the train conductor thinking, looking ahead in the dark?
Can he see in the headlights the tracks leading into an unfamiliar
land? Does he feel the heaviness of his train carrying the shame of
the world? Or does he feel lucky he's not one in the cars?

He squints and lights a cigarette.
For a moment, his face flares up, then darkness eats it again.

2.

Maria, Ioana, Stefana, Gheorghe, Ion, Constantin
came back in spring as snow crocuses.
A field of names trembling in the sun.
Step lightly, dear. Watch out for the numb bee
that lands on their tongues and sips their songs.

The line

The line in front of the store was so long it had a Line
Committee and a Line Master who kept the Line List. What is
the line for? someone asked. People shrugged: Don't know;
whatever they bring. Oranges. Chocolate. Cheese. No, it's for
toilet paper, answered the boy in front of me.

The Line Master consulted with the Line Committee and
approved the Line List. There was a line to get in Line, which got
even longer when the factory shift ended. The Line Master was
very proud. He had an important job to do. Everyone was quiet
and obeyed the Line Rules: no cutting, no pushing, and no
telling political jokes.

The president of the United States is meeting with his Chinese
counterpart at a summit on human rights.
Do you have elections? asks the U.S. president.
The Chinese president blushes and answers softly:
Yes, evely molning.

It's meat! the boy yelled, and the line rippled with excitement.
I saw the truck! Large packages. Enough for everyone!

The first Romanian astronaut leaves a note to his wife:
I'm flying in space on Soyuz. I'll be back Friday.
On Friday, he's back from space and finds a note from his wife:
I'm waiting in line for meat. Don't know when I'm back.

Here's 50 lei, the teacher said in front of the hushed first grade class. Go get me whatever they bring in that line. I hope there's meat.

What do the cannibal parents tell their children on Christmas Eve? *If you don't behave, Santa won't come this year, and we won't have any steak for Christmas.*

The light was dim. They announced they'd sell the meat through the back door. 300 people stormed to the back. The Line Committee was outrun. The Line Master fell and lost the Line List. Everyone yelled and pushed. Crushed bunions, sharp elbows, sweat. Don't get in front of me, motherfucker. I waited in line four hours. The little girl cried.

There was no meat. I walked back home with a necklace of toilet paper rolls.

The white ear

The white ear was large and a bit hairy. It sat on the table between the two red armchairs in the red-carpeted hallway, listening to everything we said. The cartilage stretched and twitched to catch every word in the house. At night, it listened to our breathing.

Through underground wires, the ear was connected to other ears in town. A city of ears, one in every apartment and several others clustered in listening offices, eavesdropping day and night.

There were noises on the line every time I called: click-click-click, and a whirr. The listening ears were bored and someone was sharpening a pencil. Someone else was grinding coffee for the long shift ahead.

My father talked to his brother and shouted into the large white ear as if he wanted to be heard across the country where Uncle Peter lived. They knew the ears were listening, so they only talked about vacation days and Grandma's hospital stays. Click-click-click-whirr: the city of ears dozed off and snored.

Other times, I talked to my long-distance boyfriend. I miss you, I whispered into the large white ear. I miss your hands, your mouth, your skin. Tick-tick. The city of ears pricked with attention. Wires snapped and whirred. I miss your lips, your tongue, I whispered. My voice echoed in the city. Tick-tock, the line answered. Tick-tock. Tick-tock.

Once a year, the large white ear rang at 6 a.m. My other uncle called from America only on New Year's Day. Startled, the city of ears rang off the hook.

Tapes turned. Typewriters typed. Files were filed. *Are you coming back this year?* my father asked, meaning *Are you coming to get us out of here?* Breathless, the city of ears waited for a response. The tapes turned. Sharp pencils hung in the air. The typewriters stopped for a while, then started again, typing the silence away.

ABOUT FLIES

They tied the man to a pole in the middle of the square, smeared his body with honey, and left him to die. Soon, clouds of flies were feasting on him, sipping honey and blood through their long straws. A young woman took pity on the prisoner and started to fan away the flies. The man opened his eyes: *Stop! Leave the flies alone. They are full and happy. If you shoo them away, other flies will take their place, hungry and thirsty, and they will kill me. So stop. You're not helping.*

Instead of hearts, the kids on my street had jars full of flies in their chests. They were holding contests: whose heart had more black flies trapped inside? My parents didn't want me to play with those kids, and all I wanted to do was run away from home and play with them. Show them my glass heart full of beautiful blue and green flies, glimmering like buzzing gems.

But they weren't flies. They were angels flying about, everywhere, clouds of angels getting into our mouths. Only we didn't know. We thought they were flies and caught them with sticky yellow tape.

THIS CRABGRASS IS NOT THE TRUTH

Nor is this dandelion, nor this clover, no matter what the bees might say. Nor is this maple tree, although it moves and glows like flame. The truth doesn't grow in grasslands and prairies. And don't tell me it grows from the bones buried in battlefields, or in forced labor camps. The truth is not a weed. It doesn't grow in the wild. The truth is wheat, and corn, and rice. It grows on the farm.

The State Agriculture Enterprise farms the truth and harvests the plants in large silos. They are cut and dried in the dark. The grain is milled into gray flour, which is mixed with water and artificial flavors into a cement-like paste. Small loaves are shaped by machines and baked into bread. At daybreak, the truth bread is delivered to the stores where crowds are waiting in line for hours: two loaves for a family of four per day, no more. The woman behind the counter checks the box on the ration card. A few crumbs fall from the truck and the ants carry them to their own crowds underground.

FOOTPRINTS

The tears have dried overnight, and salt is all that's left on the
asphalt. The sidewalk is dusted with white crystals that crunch
underfoot and sparkle in the morning sun.

I see a maze of ancestors, the footprints of everyone who walked
before me. The sidewalk wears necklaces embedded in salt. Some
are small, of children, and some are long, as if the person was
limping. Some are well defined; others are blurry, the footprints
of ghosts.

I follow them to the train station. The footprints tell me where
to go: on Wood Street, down Union Avenue to the tracks.
Through the dust of dried tears, the footprints continue out
of town.

NIGHT/DAY

Each night, the spider slept with me. He was orange with black checkers and covered me up to my chin with his woolly body. He followed me in my dreams, hanging low above my head. I was scared and wanted to run, but I couldn't move. In my sleep, he caressed my cheek with his furry paw, soft as the fringe of a cashmere blanket.

Each day the sun is born new because it burns new sky twigs. Same for the fire that burns new fuel every day, new logs. The lungs are newborn every day because they burn new air. The hair, the skin, the nails are newborn. They stretch and curl and grow. Only the beating heart is old, my dear, a boat loaded with beasts, an ark that sails the ocean forever in the dark.

THE WIND BLEW OFF ALL THE STREET SIGNS

After the storm, we woke up in a different city: all the streets and avenues named after famous figures of the past had new names like The Socialism Victory Boulevard, Steel Workers Avenue, or The People's Square. The buildings were mixed up as well: the grocery was empty, except for cheap champagne; the library was full of old shoes; someone's house was now a kindergarten; and the butcher was selling nails and screws.

We walked the streets for decades, confused, unable to find our way. We finally got used to the new names, but one night the wind came back and changed the signs again.

THE PLACES WE USED TO ROAM

I've been there, hanging out with the dwarf at the Palisades circus, and with the clown with tragic eyes smoking a cigarette on the roof of the flying Zamboni. I've been there, in another life, a memory, a photograph, a dream. There's nothing romantic about that.

And the angel perched on the statue watching us intently is actually a fat fly on the icon framed under glass in the Colentina slum, rubbing its legs and staining the Virgin Mary. And we mistakenly think we see a beauty mark on her face, or a tear.

I've been there, where the enormous slugs crawl across the sky and slime the moon. We used to tie our rowboats to the lamp posts, and they floated all night next to our windows, waiting for us to jump in. We never did.

The places we used to roam are still there. Our memories are still there, eating crepes at Luna Park by the blinking eyes of the woman with the nose rotten by rust, spinning metal cars on her skirt. There is nothing romantic about the powder sugar that falls like snow and clings to my only dress and the sour cherry syrup drop about to fall and ruin it.

The boats are still tied to the lamp posts on our street, waiting for our younger versions to jump in and row away.

WRITING ON THE WALLS AT NIGHT

My daughter stands up quickly in the bed and scribbles
something on the ceiling with a black marker. Wow, she grew so
tall, stretching to reach the ceiling. Long legs, long arms. I squint
in the dark to read, but her writing is unintelligible. When she's
done, she lies back quickly next to me, fast asleep.

The black plume of smoke seeps out from the wall. It looks like
ink floating toward me through the water. When it gets close, it
turns into a woman's face. My mother.

What is it with mothers and daughters up at 2 a.m.? We're on a
rocky beach, looking out at the murky sea. My mother walks in
front of me, wind snapping her skirt. She tells me something,
pointing at the green waves. I see her lips moving, but the boom
of the surf covers her voice.

In the girls' dorm room, Florina wrote my poems in black
marker on the four closet doors. Unintelligible scribbles,
finger-smudged, staining the laminated surface. Love poems for
lonely girls away from home.

It's all about not understanding the scribbles, the ink, the words. About being in the water, ears plugged. Eyes wide open, but not seeing. Then the archer gets up and comes to the wall. She points her arrow at me. I can see its tip against the bow, writing something in the air: *This is it*. I jump from the bed when she lets it go.

SCRATCHED AND BRUISED, WE EMERGE FROM WINTER AS AFTER A PLAGUE

We shed our skin and step out of the crusty bodies, leaving behind a tide of carcasses that disappear into the ground.

And we grow wings.

Thin and wet, we open them, spread them out in the sun, and wait.

And then we fly. There's nothing like the first flight, nothing like the feel of open air holding you up by the armpits against the wind, woo-hoo!

We spin and glide, drunk on light and song. Don't look down, dear. There's plenty of time to look down. For now, enjoy being small and free, and sink into the sky.

On the table, a porcelain teacup on a thin saucer

Each night, the moon comes to sip cool peppermint tea. She looks for her brother, but he's on the other side of the world. The moon holds the teacup in icy hands. The porcelain shines like a lighthouse.

Each day, the sun comes to sip hot rosehips tea. He looks for his sister, but she's on the other side of the world. The sun holds the teacup in his fiery hands. The porcelain burns like a furnace.

There's not much else happening. The porcelain teacup sits on the table in the silent room. Someone washes it every time, makes the tea, and pours it for the brother and sister. Silence falls, a white napkin next to the saucer. Outside, the planets hum and spin.

A BOAT MADE FROM A HALF-WALNUT SHELL

A boat made from a half-walnut shell floats on the dark waters. Inside it, the mouse scribbles something. The words flow like string from the tip of her pen which knits them into a small, triangular sail. The mouse raises the poem at the mast. Her heart is a compass pointing West. She knows nothing about what waits ahead: new land, new life, new dangers. Huge waves crash into the boat, but she knows it will keep sailing if she keeps writing.

The dandelion sonata

In our inverted umbrellas, we traveled through stormy waters without knowing the end of the journey. We placed love notes in bottles and let them float away from time to time. The sun was a red rooster; our hearts, rotating weathervanes.

We found solace in books on the bottom of the ocean. Dictionopolis, stacked high. Goldfish patrolled the streets, not granting any wishes.

There were paper boats made of dreams, or maybe of the love letters that no one read. The ink had long washed away, and the words were unreadable. The waves kept babbling *Return to sender. Destination unknown.*

Where do the love letters go when no one reads them? Why, in the love letter tree, of course, where they grow instead of leaves. In spring, they become sheet music. All the wildflowers, birds, and crickets know the notes.

Full of thorns, our hearts grew under glass cloches. They bloomed on the summer solstice. A young woman harvested their petals that very night for preserves. From sugar and water, she made simple syrup and mixed in the petals with lemon juice. She mumbled and stirred with a wooden spoon. The heart petals crystallized, and the air filled with fragrance.

Meanwhile, the woods were full of music. The pianist played the dandelion sonata, and the milkweeds followed with their flutes. *Crescendo! Crescendo!* Queen Anne banged her lace tambourine. *Fortissimo*, the horn of the moon.

IV

THE RUSSIAN HAT

WELCOME TO THE MUSEUM OF OUR LIVES

We're the curators, the visitors, and the paintings that paint themselves. The plump woman and her dog are an installation in red with purple lips. She's my best friend from high school, the one who died young of hepatitis. I trace a stripe of glistening blue on the cheek of the tall bride in black, my former French teacher. In the group, I spot Pinocchio, my math teacher, with his long nose and cropped pants. They walk around and whisper to each other. I can't join the conversation, though, because I just gave birth.

Wait a minute! the artist in a top hat says. *This* tableau *needs some snow.* He sifts flour over our heads and squirts whipped cream over the baby's ruffles. *There! It's perfect now.* The small dog yelps on two feet, balancing a teaspoon on its nose.

The next exhibit is the New York City subway. A man plays a tango on the violin, and a little girl gives me a bouquet of red flowers. Large dahlias bloom in the tunnel.

Madness, the rabbit you pull out of the magician's hat.
Or is it love?

I invite you in my cave full of candles and lions. I offer you two golden apples with glowing areolas. You're trying to decipher my poems, but can't get past the spiders on the veins. Or the areolas. Your curse is to forever detangle love's knots. Look at the bright side, though: at least my name isn't Circe.

Heaven must be
a well-lit place,

a Broadway show
full of long legs
tapping in unison.

In one of the rooms, all the clothes from the closets are thrown on the floor. Mother is kneeling on top of them, searching the pockets. *I had a $5 bill and an important note in one of the coats,* she says. *What did the note say?* I ask.

I don't remember, but it was secret and very important. Something about D-Day, and what kind of soup I was supposed to make.

In the next room, I think of summer,
of time that doesn't touch us.

Of my parents,
far, far away.

Water, blue like paint, up to our waist. You slurp the small snake
like spaghetti. *What are you doing?* I yell. *Sorry*, you say, and
regurgitate the snake's head, but couldn't cough up the tail. The
snake winks at me and swims away.

Meanwhile, night soil piles outside the windows. Mountains of
night. Our windows twinkle in the valleys, so bright, so isolated.

The next exhibit is the city, a howl of windows and walls. No
one is here, but you know that people pulsate just out of sight.
The moon plays a mean sax in the sky, and you keep looking for
the exit, but all you can find is the forest with dreams hanging
low on branches.

Two unshaven guys, dressed as Mickey and Minnie, walk down
8th Avenue, holding their large cartoon heads under their arms.

Take the moon keys and open the drawer where you keep the
baby teeth. Take the sun keys and open the drawer with

birdsong. Take the Florida Keys and open the drawer with winter: Thousands of hands clap at once.

The Russian hat

Everyone had a Russian hat in Romania. I got mine at the flea market. It was expensive, oversized and soft, with a silver sheen. There were people who said my hat was made of cat fur, that all Russian hats were, but I knew different: it was a skinned Russian bunny.

I walked through cold Romanian winters with the silver bunny curled on my head. From under it, you could only see my eyes.

My headaches grew worse with each winter. It was the hat, wrapped tightly around my head. It kept it warm, but it was heavy and squeezed my skull. I suspected it wanted to smother my thoughts in fur.

I stopped wearing my Russian hat after I got to America. After it started bellowing Russian ballads loud enough to cover the noise on 34th street: *Ochi chornyye, ochi strastnyye...*

It was embarrassing. I sold it to Ursula for 5 bucks.

Ursula was Swiss and looked very pretty in my Russian hat. She had a cat, Stanton, found on Stanton Street. On cold winter nights, the hat sang Russian army choir songs and Ursula drank vodka. Stanton, though, never learned to trust it.

THE WAY HOME

It was a strange, dilapidated city that looked a lot like Bucharest, but everyone spoke English. I was trying to find my way home, to find the subway entrance, or a bus stop. You picked me up and drove through rusty rail yards, along mountains of dirt, mangled metal, and machinery parts. I was cold. You gave me your jacket and a poetry book about salamanders. I thought you wanted to save me, but you only wanted to teach me a lesson.

Poetry doesn't save anyone, you said. *It only messes with your head.*

ON A CLEAR NIGHT

We drink and talk and drink and talk—mostly about angels, but also freedom and the cruel, cruel world. I feel warm and alive until you say I'm just another corporate slave. I take another shot of freedom.

The sky is windswept, populated only by rocks and our imagination. You pour me some more God.

It's late. I wanna go home. I have to work tomorrow, like the good slave I am.

The bar door slams behind us. The sky is full of voyeuristic angels, pointing at us, fingers lit like candles.

ONLY IN NEW YORK

The white rabbit rides a bike and stops at the traffic light. He wears black shorts printed with pursed red lips and drags behind him a sign for the penthouse bar at 250 Madison Avenue. In the sticky heat, I wonder if he has marmalade on skin under that fur. He looks at me as if he knows something I don't, and clinks the bell.

Just like us, the objects long to be together. The neckties hang out in Brooks Brothers' windows. There is a conference of umbrellas in Bryant Park; a summit of Russian hats in Brooklyn; and a shoe party at my back door.

Last night I fell into the abyss again. And I wanted you to know how deep it was, so I counted the seconds: one-one thousand, two-one thousand, three-one thousand, flying, head down, into the pit. When I got to 37, I knew I was too far to be saved.

In Herald Square, the Statue of Liberty

In Herald Square, the Statue of Liberty has lunch with the silver
man. The copper robot tells them jokes from when he used to be
golden. The statue complains that her feet hurt from
standing all day.

I wonder if she lives on Staten Island and takes the ferry home. I
imagine her lifting her skirt over puddles and nodding to the
other lady in the harbor.

I wonder if the silver man sleeps with the paint on, or if he
showers. How the paint runs off his face like mercury, revealing a
strange person in the mirror. How the bathroom glints in the
moonlight, and all the pipes shine, silvery inside, as he reaches
for the towel.

A PEACH, AN APRICOT, AND A NECTARINE PIT

In her dream, my mother plants in the ground a peach, an apricot, and a nectarine pit. The trees grow in my dreams. They send down roots that tangle my brain and spread in my body; they wrap it in branches and blood vessels. My mother comes and grafts a branch from her dream onto my small trees.

Years pass. The orchard grows tall and wide. In late winter, my father prunes the trees. In my dream, the trees bloom, petals fall, and fruits grow and ripen in the sun. In her dream, Mom picks a peach and tastes my sun.

Large as a cathedral, the pear tree at the corner of Mortimer and Elliott Place has vaulted branches that hold still the painted glass sky. When it blooms, a white cloud floats above the street. I stepped inside it last night and looked up. It was quiet and light as if the world had just begun. Mom and I were small fleas, hiding inside God's beard.

THE SKY HAS MY BROTHER'S GRAY EYES

He looks down, but doesn't see me. I'm one of the faceless in the crowd inside the *Greetings from New York* snow globe. I look up at his huge eye magnified by the glass. I can see pigeons fly in his iris.

His hand shakes the globe, and snowflakes fall over swarms of people, buses, and cars. White moths, they flutter in the air. I wanna tell him, *I'm not coming home this year* but the blizzard of moths swirls into my mouth before I can speak.

You were chasing owls out of the house

Or maybe they were bats? Inside, a small dog was whimpering like rain. The walls were lined with frying pans, and Britney Spears wanted to move in with all her friends. She threw a fit when I said no.

We had just moved into the new apartment and started to unload boxes: clothes, books, dishes, stuff. Some towels caught on fire. The flames jumped to the blue blanket I got from your mom. You rushed to put it out and took the burning box outside. *Your sleeve! Your hand!* I yelled. Then I saw in the hallway two preachers in long blue robes delivering a message from God. They smiled at me, but I couldn't hear what the message was. I tried to close the door. The hinges and lock weren't working, so I left it open.

Father and I were looking for ice cream all over town, but all the shops I knew since childhood were gone. We ended up in a building where a man in a sweaty tank top sold us a bucket of ice.

This dream is no better than the one I had last night, I complained on the way back. I could barely move my feet under the iceberg I carried. Father shrugged, sucking on an ice chip.

I WAS AGAIN IN ROMANIA

I was again in Romania, this time in a huge deserted
warehouse, walking among crates of boxes and bottles
stacked up to the ceiling. No one was around, except a large
polar bear sleeping in a corner, red baseball hat over his face.

Are you the Coca-Cola polar bear? I asked.
He pushed the cap off his eyes:

Well, yes ma'am, yes, I am, he answered in a deep
belly voice.

And where is the other polar bear, the little one?

Don't know... Somewhere 'round here, probably sleeping.
He paused, then started again:

*He's all grown up now, fat, and unemployed. This is Pepsi
country.*

I LEFT MY HOME LOOKING FOR A NEW CITY

After years of wandering, I exchanged my old cement city for a new one made of glass; the city of stray dogs for the rats' city; the beggars' city for the one of the homeless; the city smelling of urine for the one of piss.

I walk the streets, looking for the girl of my past, light-footed and happy as a bird. She's gone. The streets take me to the same squares, the same houses with the same closed doors. There is no new city. It's the same one, the one I carried inside all along.

When I see the Black Sea again, the sea will also see me. She'll open her green eyes and greet me with white horses and hammers. She'll recite my poems. She'll welcome me in her cold bosom, smile with thousands of salt teeth, and carry my name from wave to wave, for I'm her lover Ovid, the exiled.

EMPIRE STATE

I left the kingdom of caterpillars for the empire of metal worms. Here the mulberry trees are made of steel with glass leaves. They bear coins for fruits that never fall to the ground. I have to crawl and climb up, up to get some. They taste like lead and make my tongue green.

I dreamed again about the caterpillars on Grandma's porch. The garden was fuzzy and warm, and the caterpillars chewed all the leaves into an intricate lace. I took some scissors and fashioned myself a wedding dress. The caterpillars spun silk, crawled onto my head, and went to sleep. They awakened as white cabbage butterflies. I wore my lace dress and butterflies veil well into the fall, before they flew away.

THE LARGEST POST OFFICE IN THE WORLD

The largest post office in the world operates at night in an undisclosed location. The postal workers sort through sacks of dreams and nightmares and stuff them in envelopes. They divide the envelopes and packages according to zip codes and throw them on conveyor belts: mostly junk mail, fragments, hallucinations, and the occasional distorted childhood memory. On the floor below, the mailmen pick them up, fill their bags, and deliver them to thousands of bedrooms at once.

You lie in your bed in deep sleep. The mailman comes in without ringing the bell and pushes the dreams through the narrow slot in your forehead. On his way out, he picks up a lollipop from the bowl in the parlor. It's naturally-flavored with green apple.

The Secret Wishes of Recyclable Objects

I wish I were a Frisbee, the plastic milk container said, so I can feel the wind and fly, Who-hoo! Hands will grab me and throw me back, and I'll be caught by other hands, what a life! To live hand-to-wind-to-hand-to-wind-to-hand-to-wind-to-dog's mouth.

I don't care much for being thrown, the newspaper said. I'm sick of carrying the bad news and staining people's fingers with black ink. Oh, how I wish I were pulp from which a brand new sheet would be stretched and cut into a notebook page, wide-ruled. And a girl would draw her life on me, complete with sunflowers, peace signs, and a love balloon, and she'd write in the neatest script *Whatever you do, you will always have love.*

I wish I were a bike, the empty beer can said, in a bike store all the way in the country, at the end of a dusty road. A young man would buy me, and pedal so proud, as if I were Pegasus. At nightfall, he'd pick up his girlfriend and she'd climb on the metal bar and hold onto him so close, her scent in his lungs. And we'd ride to the movies in the next town over through the dark fields, under the turning spokes of the stars.

THE TINY COMEDY CLUB

I performed live in front of an audience of baby dolls and stuffed animals. They laughed so hard at my jokes their button eyes popped out and their side stitches split. Stuffing floated around the room like snowflakes. The beanie babies spilled their beans, and that's the tea.

The whole city laughed, except for two pigeons in gray uniforms who flew above the comedy club. *This is no laughing matter,* they said, and shitted solemnly in the street. *I'm going to file a report with the Department of Truth.*

Someone's comedy club is another one's outhouse, I mumbled.
Go ahead, report me! I yelled.
It's a free stuffed toys country, and the teddy bears are my witnesses!

I COME HOME LATE FROM WORK AND FEEL LIKE LISTENING TO YOUR LIFE

I slip in the record, turn up the volume, and listen, eyes closed.

You start running in your labyrinth, down the shimmering tracks. You start telling me about the bar and your friends getting *higher than the Empire State* Building. You slide through the city's narrow streets, chased by the hot needle, and the needle stabs your foot, and you stumble and bleed through turning glass doors, glass walls, glass women, faster, through corridors and hallways, faster and faster, through the grooves of the moving spiral.

And your hair is on fire. You wave your burning hands. Your shirt bursts into flames: *This is it, man. This is war.*

Run through its muddy niches, crawl through its trenches, through the dark maze, down to the spiral center, its very end. Some nights are fought like this.

I go to the kitchen, pour myself a glass of wine. The walls are narrow and slightly curved and I know someone else feels like listening to the record of my life. Carefully, he places the needle on its surface. I hear the small explosions of two specs of dust.

I go out for a walk, for a run. The street is dark and shaped like a
    spiral.

LENIN'S STATUES

They were all over Eastern Europe, in every square, pointing over our heads toward the brilliant future. Ukraine had 5,500 of them. Where did they go?

Thousands tied the gigantic statues with ropes or steel cables, pulled them down, and dragged them through the streets, chanting. Young men climbed on top and made pornographic gestures, dancing, then sawed off the arms and hands and sold them for souvenirs. They broke Lenin's goatee with hammers and struck his eyeballs with their fists. They sold the metal statues for scrap. Can you imagine the glee of melting Lenin's huge head? And turning it into something useful: wheelbarrows, shovels, and spades for digging up the past.

It turns out, some Lenin statues survived. One huge stone head without nose is hidden in a gardening toolshed. Another one lies in an abandoned construction lot, among truck tires and piles of rubble. A few others lie on their sides or face down in the dirt.

There is one in Bucharest, reclining in a cow pasture at Mogoşoaia, in the grass. It's the one that used to be in front of The Free Press House. I went out there once with a friend. All of a sudden, we heard Lenin snoring. There was a drunk on the other side, passed out in the shade of Lenin's enormous head. *The whole century was drunk*, my friend said.

KHRUSHCHEV

Khrushchev visited a pig farm, and the local reporter photographed the event. Later, at the headquarters of the newspaper, the caption of the photo was the subject of a heated discussion:

—Comrade Khrushchev among the pigs?
—Comrade Khrushchev and the pigs?
—Pigs around Comrade Khrushchev?

Up against the deadline, the editor-in-chief finally decided:
Third from the left, Comrade Khrushchev.

Of course, my friend says, you can always replace *Khrushchev* with the politician of your choice.

SIGNS THE END OF THE WORLD IS NEAR (TIME TO MOVE TO NEW JERSEY)

Mother and I walk through the woods, and a woman with a twirling umbrella shows up, dressed as a clown from the Zamboni Circus. She's telling me a message, but I'm distracted by her umbrella and don't understand. A dog comes by—and it's my little brother. I recognize his eyes, the way he looks at me. He's limping, so I carry him home. Giant fires light up the sky. We're on the highway near my hometown: the hills are burning.

In Times Square, Jesus is eating Pad Thai for lunch, and a bunch of Elmos are joining the armed forces. A recent transplant from the 9th Circle of Hell chats with an old lady in the subway. She can't hear anything because Spiderman is playing the saxophone. In the tunnel, someone detonates a teapot bomb by accident. Everyone runs but the sax player.

In Bushwick, the local artist takes her peacock for a walk. The Queen Bee is walking tigers on Broadway on a golden leash. And my neighbor is walking a white dog named Noon and a black one named Midnight. He smokes and stops to pick up after them. He has a cat named Insomnia at home.

At Starbucks, the latte costs 39 bucks. The barista is wearing a
Putin T-shirt and a Karl Marx beard. He speaks with a strong
Russian accent and writes *Comrade Claudia* on the cup.
e.e. cummings is eating a freedom omelette with freedom fries
for breakfast. I pay for the latte and sit at the table with Lord
Byron. He's holding a toy bus in his hand and says, *God bus you.*

The walls are covered with portraits of Justin Bieber and
Beyoncé. On the black-and-white TV, Wolf Blitzer announces
that Beyoncé has just won the presidential elections. One should
always ask: At the end of the world, what would Beyoncé do?
She'd move the White House to New Jersey.

WHAT HAPPENS IN THE POEM
STAYS IN THE POEM

Take a dream vacation to your beautiful pain. Enjoy its five-star hotels, fine dining, and dazzling nightlife. Find new romance under your heart's Eiffel Tower and play the penny slot machines. Slide your tokens inside the wounds and pull the handle until the three cherries align. Pound after pound of shiny poems will pour out. Don't delay—book your trip today. It will be the experience of a lifetime.

Acknowledgments

Grateful acknowledgment is made to the editors of the following journals, zines, and anthologies where some of these poems first appeared, sometimes in earlier versions:

Blue Fifth Review, The Bicycle Review, Cake Magazine, Cease, Cows, Contrary Magazine, Dressing Room Poetry Journal, Dwarf Star Anthology, elsewhere, Former People, Gone Lawn, Ideomancer, Instigatorzine, JMWW, Levure Littéraire, Literary Orphans, Mad Hatters' Review, Narrative Northeast, Otoliths, Poem of the Week, Postcard Poems and Prose, Prick of the Spindle, Red Ochre Lit, Red Paint Hill, Red Rose Review, The Red Wheelbarrow, Steel Toe Review, Suitcase of Chrysanthemums Anthology, Unbroken, Up The Staircase, Uut Poetry, Vine Leaves, and *Word Riot.*

The poem *The Museum Is Closing, the Custodian Said* was inspired by photographs in the book *Self Portrait with Cows Going Home* by Sylvia Plachy (Aperture, 2004).

The poem *The Places We Used to Roam* was inspired by the photography of David Donaldson.

The poem *I come home late from work and feel like listening to your life* uses one line from the song *We Are Young* and two lines from the song *Some Nights* by Fun.

Several poems from the section *There Were No Magic Beans* were written as responses to poems from Pablo Neruda's *The Book of Questions*.

Australian filmmaker Jutta Pryor turned the poem *The Large Moth That Flew In* into a videopoem. Many thanks, Jutta.

To Ionut and Dana, va iubesc.

About the Author

Claudia Serea's poems and translations have been published in *Field, New Letters, Prairie Schooner, Notre Dame Review, The Malahat Review, The Puritan, Oxford Poetry, Asymptote,* and elsewhere. She is the author of five other poetry collections and four chapbooks, most recently *Twoxism,* a collaboration with visual artist Maria Haro (8th House Publishing, 2018). Serea's poem *My Father's Quiet Friends in Prison, 1958-1962* received the *New Letters* Readers Award. She won the *Levure Littéraire* Award for Poetry Performance, and she was featured in the documentary *Poetry of Witness* (2015). Serea's poems have been translated in French, Italian, Arabic, and Farsi, and have been featured in *The Writer's Almanac.* Her collection of selected poems translated into Arabic, *Tonight I'll Become a Lake into which You'll Sink,* was published in Cairo, Egypt, in 2021. Serea is a founding editor of *National Translation Month,* and she co-hosts The Red Wheelbarrow Poetry Readings in Rutherford, NJ.

ABOUT THE PRESS

Unsolicited Press is rebellious much like the city it calls home: Portland, Oregon. Founded in 2012, the press supports emerging and award-winning writers by publishing a variety of literary and experimental books of poetry, creative nonfiction, fiction, and everything in between.

Learn more at unsolicitedpress.com. Find us on twitter and instagram.